GRIOT

Acknowledgements:

Writers Without Borders gratefully acknowledge the support received from Birmingham City Council, Department of Leisure & Culture. We are particularly grateful for the funding which has enabled us to publish this book and for help with promoting it. Thanks go especially to Jagwant Johal (Equalities & Strategy) and Anu Singh (Libraries).

Special thanks go to David Dabydeen, Stewart Brown and Adrian Blackledge for their words of encouragement and support.

Most of this writing would not have been possible without the encouragement of our families, friends and partners – people who provide us with inspiration and understanding and who do the washing-up while we think about more important things. We may not say so very often but we truly value the fact that you are there for us.

And finally a big thank you to Nicholas Underwood for the wonderful drawing of the Iron Man, by Anthony Gormley, which leans enigmatically at the top of New Street, Birmingham.

GRIOT

Edited by Kampta Karran
and Cathy Perry

Writers Without Borders

First published 2001
by
Writers Without Borders
22, Margaret Grove,
Harborne,
Birmingham B17 9JH
Tel: (0121) 426 6413

Set in Times New Roman by Writers Without Borders
Printed by Print Plus, Birmingham

ISBN: 0953968111

Contents:

Introduction

The word Griot, the title of the collection, is West African in origin but finds parallels in almost every civilisation. The Griot is the cultural custodian, a member of a very special caste, who chronicles the history of her/his society and who can recite that collective memory when called upon. Poets in many ways perform a similar role. This collection testifies to the multicultural remembrances that have found a common home in Britain yet simultaneously live elsewhere and everywhere.

The poets whose work makes up this collection are part of Writers Without Borders, a group originally formed with the aim of welcoming writers newly arrived in the West Midlands. This meeting offers a comfortingly warm embrace that facilitates the reciprocal sharing of work and experiences in a safe and nourishing environment. These poets could be seen as a representation of wider society in microcosm. The refugee and the resident, the published and the unpublished, the old and the young, women and men, the known and the unknown all find common ground in this present endeavour.

Variety in subject, theme, form and language is a defining feature of this collection as are the different ethnic and national backgrounds of the contributors. It will appeal to specific communities and at the same time transport the reader through a world of difference and diversity. However, there are common ideas running through many of the poems. These include issues of identity, of alienation and being different, of being separated from home, of being socially and psychologically displaced and of death and rebirth. Even the works of the English writers demonstrate that it is quite possible to feel isolated and alone in one's indigenous homeland.

Although most of us live in Britain and write in English we emphasise that, while English is our meeting point, it is not the only language for self-expression in this country. Good writing crosses all borders and, in a sense, poetry itself is our country. Some of the poems published here are written in languages other than English. A few, though not all, are accompanied by translation thus making them accessible to English-only readers. There are other poems, however, that are not translated or transliterated. These will be treasured and enjoyed by many people whose rich culture embraces more than one language.

The inspiration for this collection came from an evening of poetry held at the Library Theatre, Birmingham in July 2000. A universal spirit of community emerged during and after the performances. While this anthology marks and celebrates that event, it has wider significance as a community arts project. While writing and performing poetry could be seen as an end in itself, the poetry presented here carries the diverse narratives of lived and imagined realities unfolding in a multicultural space. Grouped together, the writing takes on an added dimension providing us with interpretations that will assist in our search and our arrival at a more holistic appreciation of life. The writers' enormous creativity provides a mirror and a chant to our ancestors, ourselves and to our children.

Kampta and Cathy, May 2001

Some of the 'Writers Without Borders'

Roi Kwabena

Roi was born in Trinidad and Tobago in 1956. His work has been acclaimed in Europe, Afrika and the Caribbean where he has lectured and conducted workshops on historic themes at many universities, schools and cultural venues. Between 1992 and 1994 he served as a Senator in Trinidad and Tobago's Upper House of Parliament. A collection of his parliamentary debates has been published.

'open mike' will be published in Roi's collection *as long as* which is due later this year. The other poems were originally published in Roi's collection *Whether or Not* and his spoken word CD *Y42K*.

Apparitions

Bags of donated grain being
dispensed from the sky
by iron birds. Frail

tribal peoples on a trek
to no where. Civil war unabated
for thirty years, though the media
reports fifteen.

Helpless refugees on
a London bus, confide their disgust.
Now the church reclaims
chains that scorch
our memories.

Mid-day, just like *j'ouvert*
an illegal street party in *brum*.
Police don their riot gear
while european youth play
african drums and *moko jumbies*
prancing in the spring sun.

What response
can I muster in these trying times. An
impressed friend reports
of the rebels' victory,
yet I am not encouraged.

Forgive us our debts
(for the Jubilee 2000 Foreign Debt Campaign)

wish we had a father
not only in heaven
but also on earth

we would forgive
our debtors
and all those who
trespassed against us

the genocide ...
the chattel slavery ...
the indentureship ...
the religious conversion ...
the plunder of our antiquities ...
the economic deprivation ...
the scientific exclusion ...

could we expect
our debts to be forgiven
so that we may feed our people

we won't be led into
military aggression
we will uphold the ideals
of tolerance and equality

we will fair trade
all commodities
we will promote
sustainable development
and protect
our earth's environment

oh! can we expect
our debts to be forgiven
as we adhere to principles
that will be beneficial to all of humanity

we the rich-but-considered-poor nations
of the southern hemisphere ...

no hearts

gone
are the days
of puppets, robots
and bionic-men

these tales
are of nations ruled by
ones who appear as humans
and with considerable intelligence,
yet show no emotions ...

being manipulated from afar by
some who feign compassion
with plans for further destruction ...

my son enjoys these comics.

open mike

new poets
read their work

confidence worn on
shoulders
to carry such a burden
this eternal sensitivity
with struggle to
tell
record
defend
applaud
protest
remember
be heard

be seen
be believed

".. my work is evolving .."
a young bright mind confided

Shail Agrawal

Born in Varanasi in India's year of independence, Shail graduated with a MA in English literature from Benares Hindu University, Varanasi, at the age of 20. Her other interests include painting, story writing, music and philosophy. She has been resident in the UK since the age of 21 and only recently re-started writing. A member of The Cannon Poets, Geetanjali Multilingual Group, and Katha, London, her first books are "Samidha", "Offerings of thought" and "Neti-Neti", "Not this" will be published in 2001.

She can be contacted at shailagrawal@hotmail.com

Dawn

Once again a hustling-bustling day
has sacrificed itself on the altar of night.
In this still of darkness, bolting my eyelids,
I search for peace and solitude. But where?

These silent moments bursting with memory
have many tales to tell. The hermit heart
has come back from exile with its begging bowl.
Once again I donate myself. But how?

This eagle of memory soaring high
causes many ripples, stirs many waves
piercing the pathway to my mind.
Once again I let it fly. But why?

All these anchored boats ready to voyage
in this sea of never-land tomorrow
stand marooned because a fresh wind dawn
beacons the odyssey of a brand new day once more.

On the Pavement

Uncombed, unshaven, unclean
in a tattered, oversized-coat
he was always there
timeless and old.

A red burning face, fatigued
greying in patches, listless
like a burnt-up coal.
Muddy sticky eyes, unyielding
gazing nowhere in particular
from his cardboard blanket.

An empty beer bottle
his only possession
close to the chest
rendered no warmth.

A dead crowd rushing, passing by
did not know how to help or stop
this overflow of homeless destitute.

A lady from a van stretched the soup-cup
but the street-urchin did not move.
All his strength spent up, fighting
the battle of hunger and loneliness
with bitterly numb fingers and a frosted heart.

She put the spoon on his dry
stiff curled-up tongue
When a sob choked and died
on the pavement that night,
"Many times I tried to finish it all"

A silent tear slipped from his eyes
and drowned my soul.

Refugee

When the sky is not theirs
the earth and sea are a foreign land
Under the shadow of the darkest cloud
they shatter into a fleeing slumber.

Obstinate thoughts hammer and pierce
the silence of a fragmented wall
Unable to dream, dwell or ponder
those tired limbs just surrender.

But a big but, a snake of a question
hisses, cajoles and shakes again
How long – Where – When
Can you tell – Do you know –

How far is the peace --------
the place we once called home
to a frightened infant; a doting mother
a helpless father and the lull of a storm?

Promise Me Not

The moon,
a slice of bread
shimmers bright in the sky.
Stars, my hungry children
scavenge
for that half eaten loaf
thrown in disdain.
A gift, a loan, a master plan
A bondage of slavery
for generations to come.
This on-going battle
between have and have-nots.
Where is the saviour
to rewrite the lot.
I am the sad barren face
of a so called third-world nation
An ugly dry patch
On an otherwise lush velvety earth
Even my babies are born
with a begging bowl in their hands
shackled and chained to it.
A bowl so big and bottomless
that it has swallowed
all our hands and legs
Faceless, crippled
my parched and arid race
sits and waits like the dry earth
with a crack in its heart
watching those merciful clouds float by

Yet again they gather and hover
over a bleak horizon.
These distraught images
of flea infested eyes
of barely skin clad bones
so called childhood in dying arms
flashes in front of the world.

Promise me not-----------
to throw just a few pennies more
and then forget it all.

Rod Dungate

Rod moved from London to Birmingham in 1984 and reckons it was the one decision in his life that he got right. He splits his time between writing – he's a playwright, poet and journalist – and working as an education and training consultant specialising in creativity and personal presentation.

Unknown Lands

You gave me a rose so very red,
No need for words, the words you said,
But I am afraid to understand —
I grasp the thorns, they pierce my hand
And our time hangs suspended on a scarlet thread.

Warning lights pulse in my head,
Morning skies fill my heart with dread,
Living flesh resolves as sand,
Your rose is so very red.

So what of autumn when flowers are shed
In spring new buds bloom in their stead,
In danger zones lives can expand,
Red door leads to an unknown land,
When a flower sleeps it isn't dead
Your rose is so very red.

Late Night Final

Turning his collar up against complaining sky,
Hunched against chill wind, debilitating drizzle,
Against this year's early started spring
Which scuttled away today, no warning,
He treads, at steady pace, up New Street
Knowing the City lies in wait for the evening:
Where flower stall stood, flowers drown,
He sees them, hears call on fading air
Newspaper seller from his cold metal coffin:
Late night final: late night final.

City wraiths hover at several bus-stops,
Drift Rotundawards, to Bull Street, Moor Street Station,
He sees them tonight and every night, Monday to Friday,
Some hushed shadow play, week in, week out,
Same, except when sun is shining, why then
Much more clearly he sees his world, and bigger,
Big Mac polystyrene box, one dropped earring,
One trampled Evening Mail gasping its last,
Same cry, fitful, sliding between worlds,
Late night final: late night final.

He turns, on auto-pilot, up Needless Alley,
Fall back two centuries, night before, night before,
Some shelter here from wind, though walls close in,
He sees from dim descending stairs, deep music
Beat its path to outside world, pass by;
Girl, urgent on mobile, fails to meet her classmate,
Two more, shivering in skimpy, thin-strap dresses,
Join the fray, mouths dark with laughter,
He sees, the evening could start here, he passes by,
Late night final: late night final.

Into Temple Row, cross Cathedral Square,
Cobbles grimed with development, dull polished shoes,
No street lights echo off antique glistening tombs,
Not in grey middle time before night falls,
He does not experience God as he treads the Square,
He sees boy with girl in bank doorway
Young love: boy croons This is the end of our affair;
On Ernest Harper, Eighteen-Seven deceased
Pigeons scrap for discarded cone of chips;
Late night final: late night final.

Treading at steady pace down Colmore Row
To Snow Hill Station – destination Smethwick Galton
                                    Bridge,
He sees, not man who greets his waiting friend,
Touch on elbow, shared look that says it all,
But, in his mind, his painstakingly plotted garden,
Much admired by neighbours passing by,
And newly fitted kitchen, though he never cooks,
He wonders what's in Radio Times tonight (being
                                    Thursday)
Or tomorrow night; for weekend, he knows there's
                                    nothing....
Late night final: late night final.

Not Much of a Choice

Transportation of live animals is an established
Controversial cross-channel trade;
Sometimes it makes headlines in the news:
Tempers run high, some say out of proportion,
Some say facts are obscured by misinformation,
Others that animals like us have a different concept of
                                                    suffering,
Some that the trade should be changed from on hoof to
                                                    on hook,
Not much of a choice, is it?

Travelling conditions are usually bad
Over-crowding, rations restricted (if any at all)
By law there's supposed to be regular watering
But no-one's heart's really in monitoring,
Better, say the pure-in-heart, to stop the trade quickly:
If rogue traders are caught they pay well heavy penalties
But their prizes are huge when we slip through the net,
Not much of a choice, is it?

So I made the journey across the English Channel
Worse than a cattle truck, but how was I to complain?
We were crammed in like sardines,
There was no watering,
It was hard to breathe it was so hot;
Rations were restricted to tomatoes
And fifty-eight of my fellow-travellers didn't make it:
Not much of a choice, was it?

Unlocking

A long day and late home: sharp wind and drizzle in the
air,
Through my thin jacket a sharp pinch from a reluctant
English spring;
A weary turning of the five-lever mortice; a stooping for
the bottom lock.
And then the sudden shock of it.
On the chill night air the most fragile scent
So natural I'd nearly passed it by:
A long time I stood, idiot-like, at my front door
Not even trying to make sense of it,
An unruly clump of rocket planted the year before.

When I was eighteen, reaching home one summer night,
I was halted in front of the house
By the heady scent of honey-suckle growing at the back:
That night in my youth I sang out loud.

Tonya J. Bolton

Tonya is a 23 year old English-born graduate of Jamaican descent. She has been writing all her life. Taking inspiration from black writers such as Alice Walker and Nora Zeale Hurston, her poetry, essays and short stories examine the complex issues of race, gender and spirituality. She is currently working on her M.A. and writing her first book of poems.

Butterfly Woman

I give birth to myself,
Like a butterfly emerging
Out of its crystal cocoon.
Struggling to escape my claustrophobic case
I fight for freedom.
Pushing down on the pain
I reach up to the light called life
And flutter my new crumpled wings in joy.

But I am more than just a delicate beauty,
I am more than just female anatomy,
I am more than the black skin which covers my flesh
Like an apple I have a core
Containing the seeds of my spiritual self.
All these qualities are celebrations of God's ingenuity
Yet are worthless in man's society.

Captured and crushed to death for their pleasure
I am put on display as a pressed butterfly.
My wings are pinned down while I'm still alive,
Crucified, I realise that I cannot survive.
I scream out from within my glass prison
But no-one hears me.
My exterior shell is all they choose to see.

I AM

I am Alpha and Omega, the First and the Last.
I am the Future, the Present and Past.
I alone hold the keys to the gates of Heaven and of Hell,
It's up to you to decide where You will dwell.
So do not behave with the IQ of a dumb ass,
For the Words I have written will soon come to pass.

I am the unmoved Mover
The Most High, Jah Jehovah.
I am your only Saviour
And I abhor all ungodly behaviour.
It was I who destroyed your Tower of Babel,
For My Omnipotence is neither fake nor fable

I loved you so much that I granted you Free Will.
In return you steal, kill and commit evil.
Like Doubting Thomas you people never believe
And yet wonder why you never receive.
Will you only acknowledge Me when you feel the heat of
                                                    Hell?
By then it will be too late to reclaim the soul you now
                                                    sell.

I am Endless, Changeless, Timeless and above your
                                                    reason
For it was I who created the Earth and its seasons.
So whilst you joke around and jeer
The destruction of Babylon draws near.
Do not permit your spirit to be damned
By denying who I AM.

None are Worthy

When I think of you my whole being becomes glad
And no longer am I suicidal or sad.
I owe everything to you,
Thank-you, Lord, for seeing me through.
Sometimes I feel as though I am not worthy of your Love
But if I were perfect you would not have come down
                                                    from above.
For you came, not for the righteous, but for sinners,
To transform the losers of this life into winners.
Blessed are the poor, the sick and needy,
Woe unto them who are proud and greedy.
Blessed are they who are meek and mild,
Those who are pure in heart like a child.
Woe unto them who claim to know religion
Yet possess no spiritual vision.
Woe unto the people who are prejudiced,
For hatred grows inside them like a cancer cyst.
Woe unto those who preach moral correctness on a
                                                    Sunday,
While with their neighbour's wife do they secretly lay.
Woe unto those who think themselves better than others,
Those who judge their sisters and brothers.
Let he who is without sin cast the first stone,
For none are worthy to sit on the Almighty's throne.

Same Old

You were the wolf in sheep's clothes
Who tried to devour a Nubian rose,
Distorting yourself as you propose.
I, like an ox going to the slaughterhouse to die,
Let you suck my blood and bones 'til dry.
Our union went from bad to much, much worse
As though it were under an evil voodoo curse.

The roundabout relationship spun round and around,
Never really taking off from the ground,
As respect, trust and honesty were qualities I never
                                                found.
I grew tired of your lying,
And sick of my spirit dying.
So I gave up on you, as staying
Would mean a lifetime of me obeying.

To this day you haven't a clue
Of the emotional rape you put me through.
You often said I must feel since I can't be told,
I'd like to see you try now I'm big and bold.
You used to say I was callous and cold
But over my life you no longer have any hold.
You and I are not of the same mould
For you will always be the same old.

Same old shit, same old pain.
That's why I'd never take you back again.
Same old shit, same old pain.
I refuse to let a man drive me insane.
Losing you was my great gain,
For I'll never allow myself to be abused again.

Things between us got well out of hand,
I was sinking fast into your quicksand.
I had to escape to find fertile land
And from my life you are now banned.
Its about time rusty chains were broken
For blind eyes have finally awoken.

I've learnt the lesson in my mistake,
And summoning all my strength I make a complete
                                        break.
I'd whip your ass if I were a man,
And ask you if you thought you were Peter Pan.
You and I belong firmly in the past,
For our rocky foundation wasn't built to last.

Milorad Krystanovich

Milorad was born in Ramljane, Croatia and studied Serbo-Croat language and Yugoslavian literature at Split University. He has worked as a language and drama teacher, a librarian and as a stage director. Milorad has been writing in Serbo-Croat since 1975 and in English since 1994.

'Mirror Writing', 'Lullaby' and 'Correspondence' were translated from Serbo-Croat in collaboration with Cathy Perry.

'Outside the Coma' and 'Mirror Writing' were first published in Milorad's collection *Easel and Ashes*.

Outside of the Coma

A mime actor, afraid of door bells
Returned to his home:
There was time but not a space
For the symmetry of his footprints.

The sound of an unzipping suitcase
Echoed through a flannel silence:
There was no entry visa to go
Into the slow motion of his childhood.

An orange glow, the only light
From the level of a streetlamp:
His hands, freed from a pair of gloves
Were reflected in the glass of a porch.

The flowers in a vase seen through
A bay window made him feel indoors:
What kept his voice distant
And his movements stranded by the house?

A car disappearing into the corner
Of the darkness piled up above a street:
He could not hum to repeat
The tune of wind chimes from upstairs.

The sky moved in the colour
Of deep blue matching the roses at the gate:
His heart, plugged in to a kite
Received a present – the night burden of air.

Odslikom Pisati

Dnevnik za sve riječi
Potonuo mi u bole
Ali više ne
Jezik tih stranica
Spaljen
Govor usahao
U naliv-peru
Mojim obmanama natočenim
Na praznini
Staklene te površine
Stvaram novi ritam
Otisnut u zrak
Dubinom svakog daha
U sunčevini i plavom
Otkinutom iz odraza
Neba Engleskog
I otpalim s golubice
Sivim perom
Dotičem pepeo u tintarnici

Mirror Writing

A diary for all the words
I used in the past
But no more
The pages and the language
Burnt
Words dried
In a pen filled
With the diarist's illusions
On the emptiness
Of a glass surface
I create a new rhythm
Forcing it into the air
A thin thread
Of sunlight and blue
Pierces the reflection
Of an English sky
I touch the grey feather
Shed by a dove
The inkwell is filled with ash

Uspavanka

Tad i sad – isto disanje,
duboki talog vazduha
u zavičaja zavežljaju:
svoda napuknut luk udahnuti se ne može.

Besumna krila – gvozdeno perje
osuto iz tog razornog leta.
   Svaki mi dah iznova puca u opni
   moje uspavanke za tebe.

Avioni ne daju ti usnuti,
ne mogu te ni podijiti milo dijete,
nit' otvoriti se mogu
tvoje vjedje u kolijevci nesanice.

I tada i sada – sjenke,
granate što vidaju zadrhtalo tlo,
zemlju – neuzoranu, nezasijanu,
ranu u zipci otsutnog mi pogleda.

Lullaby

Now as then – breathing is the same.
A sediment of native air lies
heavy in the bundle of home: the sky's
shattered arc can hold no more.

Outstretched wings shed iron
feathers in unearthly, silent flight.
       With every sigh the waters of
       My lullaby will break anew.

       The planes cannot hush you,
       I cannot feed you, little one and still
       Your eyes will not stay open in
       The cradle of your wakefulness.

And now as then the shadows come,
grenades that shake the unhealing ground –
a land not ploughed, not sown,
a wound open in the anguish of my eyes.

Dnevnicki zapis

Drveće i brdo izbivaju
tek u zatvorenim očima:
te još odavno ne svrate zvijezde,
hrapavo od oblaka, otud izmiče i nebo.

Samo po kriški Mjeseca
da se razabrati noć
u podne: *mjesečina gle,*
kroza danje svjetlo ukazuje svoj veo.

Zrcaliti se u vlastitom pogledu
nametnula si svijetu: trajati
po rubovima tudjih udisaja
ne približuje te tvome zavičaju.

        Pogledaj oko sebe:ljudi
umiru otrovani ljepotom;
ako ih glasom otkriješ u beskraju,
šapatom odjekuju no tvoje riječi.

Samo po otiscima slova
može se pronaći pismo u koverti
na ruci tvojoj: *prijateljice čuj,*
život se prevodi u smrt a ne obrnuto.

Correspondence

Tree-line and hill now live
Only behind closed eyes –
This year even the stars have gone,
Storm clouds obscure the skies.

Only in the thin bright crescent
Can noon remember night –
Look, through the sunshine
A veil of moon's soft light.

She sees the world only through
The reflections in her eyes:
Safer to dream of that far country
Than breathe home's bright realities.

Look around you: people
Die poisoned by beauty; if your voice
Can reach into the emptiness
Their whispers may echo your words.

Only a few faded lines
Of the letter in her hand remain:
My dear friend, hear me, Life
Is translated into Death but never back again.

Cathy Perry

Cathy started writing in 1999. She is fascinated by poetry translation and has worked with Milorad and with Soran on the translations of their poetry. She is a member of The Cannon Poets.

Missed Connection

Reflected lights
run a senseless journey
round the red-framed window
the café is suspended
bright against the night
inside the glass each traveller
guards his space
pretends he is alone
watches smoke blossom
over an ashtray
outside
the darkness looks away.

Behind tired eyes
another image hovers –
your face as I first saw it
and the thin steam rising.

Tate Modern

There is one red boat on the river
One bird in the sky
One birch leaf shimmering in the wind
On the wall one painting, one colour
In the crowd one man
One hand to touch my hand
One beginning with one end
Just one red boat on the river

Haiku

In a jewelled cage
      little green bird caught between
          sun and candlelight.

Shadows on the lake -
      a seagull paints the ice with
          one long orange leg.

Lone seagull on the
      river wall - the call of home
          rises with the tide.

First light. Pale lime leaves
      dance outside the window but
          the sky is heavy.

Denniston Stewart

Denniston is a 44-year-old mature student who has just graduated from University. He has been writing poetry for as long as he can remember. He is essentially a performance poet. The themes of his work are mainly social issues and children. Much of his work is done in patois and he makes no apologies. Denniston has had some work published and regularly performs at venues throughout the West Midlands as well as workshops in schools.

Constantly Flowed

Constantly flowed
The stream of our presence,
We the descendants of diverse
nations of people, languages and cultures
We have stamped our mark on this society
economically and socially,
We are the roots of the future.
Our histories have been intertwined,
From the beginning of time,
yours and mine
Let us forget not the memory of all
the heroes of our past
Let us give honour,
To whom honour is due
Let us honour the memory
Of those who lost their lives,
In the many wars, battles and skirmishes
The million of Indian soldiers
Behind the front lines,
Distinguished men of valour
Men from the West Indies and African regiments,
Whose stories were never told?
Let us honour those who have overcome,
Obstacles socially and politically
And can now stand tall
Icons for one and all
Politicians, Union Leaders, Community leaders, Nurses,
Writers, Sportsmen and the workers who man the factory
floors
Continue to play their part,
At the heart of every community.

Let Us Now!

Let our cultures
transcend
The barriers and
boundaries of race
Let us share the
inheritance of this vast
world
Let the richness of our
cultures
Blend like aromatic
spices our hearts and
minds
Let us bask in the hope
of a utopia
Where equality reigns
supreme
Let us join hands and
hearts
And seek the ties that
bind us together
Let us drink freely from
the cup of equality
Let us appease ourselves
of its fruits equally
Let justice shine like the
midday sun
And let the bells of
freedom
Ring freely throughout
the land
And the sweet songs of
joy and peace
Echoes on, and on, and
on…

Windrush

It was 1948
On de Windrush Ship
500 men fram de Caribbean
de pon it
fram warme Jamaica san
to dis cole Inglish lan
we spen twenty eight deys
pon de Windrush Ship
an meny of us did feel real sick
cudent tek de tossing
a de Windrush Ship
so wen we ear lan ahoy
ever bady pack up
dem wan likkle grip.
De ship dack a Tilbry
evrywan begin fe feel merry
settin fut inna de Madda Cuntry.
lukin roun it wus ent very jally
noh wha we did imag gine
de weda wus dan
we bar gin far
de scene luk drab and glumy
wid plenty chim knee
wey luk laka factry
soh we step pan
de hallowed British Sile
and luk farwud to a futtar
we dreamt wud be betta
on our Hinglish Adventsha
fah meny de yeas were ruff
in fack, it was ruff and tuff
evry wear we wente
what a spec tikle
ow we suvive God nose

it was a mirakle
we cud get noh pleace fe res
ar eds a likkle
in ar Madda Cuntry Brittin
fe all a wee de futa was uncer ten
NO DAUGS, NO IRISH, NO BLACKS
some start fe wuk all de
owers God giv ven
jus fe mek a livin
an fe put a wey a kupple shillin
meny chrow a cupple han a pardna
but life still gat garda
start suffa race ism inna hevry quarta
wan an too get charge fe murder
defendin demself from de attacka
whuse weapans, bicycle chein,
winkle picker, knuckle dusta
but still we hole we carna
an from de draw a de pardna
we start fe get we life in arda
pay a depasit to de banka
fe we own little spat
and dat was dat.
Tings tek a wile fe get betta
thru meny art aches
we add to suffa
wile dey kep deir stiff uppa
but dis wus jus
a chapta cause
afta fifty yeaz we remba
de gud an de bad
de happy and de sad
of life in de Madda Lan
equality we neva add
appar tunity we didn't get
so now in owa children
we av owa opes and our dremes

44

we de pion ears ave laid
a salid foundashun inna Britten
tru blood, sweat and tearz
in de eat and de cole
deres noh streets fill wid gole!
jus a sto ree, we were tole
the gole is the jewil dat's inside
develup tru
de sufferin fiars of time
so fifty years ago
or fifty more to cum
we remba de Empia Winrush
wen she furst cum.....

My Child

My child, the apple of my eye
For you I'll try and try
To grow you well
Teach you how to read and spell
And did I grow you well?
Only time will tell

My child the apple of my eye
For you I'll try and try
In you lay all my dreams and wishes
So grow my child grow

My child the apple of my eye
For you I'll try and try
To plant in you the seeds of love
To treat everyone fairly and equally

My child the apple of my eye
For you I'll try and try
In you flows the blood of heroes
Freedom-fighters, martyrs of the cause
Fight on my child
And did I grow you well?
Only time will tell

My child the apple of my eye
For you I'll try and try
To instil in you the good values of this life
In you our destiny lies
So reach my child, reach for the skies

Untold!

Untold is our story
Omitted from the pages of history
Invisible and silent
The acts of our bravery
The unnamed millions who gave their lives freely
In the battle for freedom and democracy
Unheard of, the 14 Indian regiments,
Those lions of war on the Western Front
No mention of the countless casualties
Who in the trenches lay?
Untold is their story, omitted from the pages of history
The regiments from the Caribbean Islands
Airmen merchant seamen, munitions men
The British West Indian Regiment
Who fought far and wide?
The Kings African Rifles, who went to battle with pride
Unseen is their presence on remembrance days
While the bugle blows a tune for the Unknown Soldier
And another wreath gets laid
While the memory of whole generations of people
From the Empire is untold
Omitted from the pages of history…

Sayyara Nayyer Syed

Sayyara was born in Pakistan and migrated to the UK in the early '70s. She received her education in both England and Pakistan and later came to teach as a lecturer in a further education college. She has a great desire and love for poetry and has been writing Urdu poetry for over ten years. Sayyara lives with her two daughters who give her inspiration for her poetry.

غزل

چراغ سورج کو دکھاتے کیوں ہو
ناداں آگ پانی میں لگاتے کیوں ہو

اے عشق میں ہے دھواں دھواں ہونا
سلگنے دو ، شمع کو بجھاتے کیوں ہو

موجوں کی روانی سے خفا ہونا کیسا
طوفانوں میں ٹھہراؤ چاہتے کیوں ہو

جن کے ہاتھوں سے کاسئہ وفا ٹوٹ گیا
پھر ان کے آگے ہاتھ پھیلاتے کیوں ہو

شب کے آنچل میں سہمی سہمی سی تنہائی
ہوئی سحر کہہ کہہ کے ڈراتے کیوں ہو

اشکوں کی برسات میں کون ڈوب گیا
اس راز سے پردے اٹھاتے کیوں ہو

چاند راتوں کو تم نے بے خواب کیا
دن کی آنکھوں سے خواب چراتے کیوں ہو

غیروں کی غلامی کو لبیک کہہ تم نے
خود کو اب آزاد کراتے کیوں ہو

سربیا ہو کہ چیچنیا یا فلسطین و کشمیر
بے گناہوں کا خون بہاتے کیوں ہو

سیارہ نیر سید

ہجرتوں کے عذاب

نثری نظم

گاؤں اک عجیب تھا   مسافتوں کی دھول سے   دن تھے بیمار کے
بانجھ اس کے کھیت تھے   اتنے پڑے تھے راستے   خواب کے خمار کے
اور پانی اس کے کنویں کا   اجنبی فضائیں سی   دھنک کے سب رنگ تھے
یمار کا طبیب تھا   ساتھی کوئی، دور نہ قریب تھا   بہت سہما وقت تھا

وہاں کا ایک شخص تھا   ماں کی دعا تھی ساتھ میں   اچھی اس کی جاب تھی
دولت بیشمار تھی   اور خدا کی ذات بھی   بہت لمبی سی کار تھی
شہرت اس کے پاس تھی   بہن کا پیار تھا   اور سوئمنگ پول والا
لیکن مزاج اسکا غریب تھا   اور بے وطنی اسکا نصیب تھا   محل نما مکان تھا

دھرتی پہ اسکا پاؤں تھا   پھر دیس نئے وہ آ گیا   نئی ہر اک بات تھی
سوچ افق کے پار تھی   موسم اسکا سرد تھا   نئی ہی زبان تھی
ستاروں سے اسکی دوستی   لوگ تو برے نہ تھے   نئے اس کے یار دوست
اور چاند اسکا رقیب تھا   پر مزاج انکا برف تھا   اور نیا اس کا مقام تھا

اگ آیا اسنے درخت تھا   ملیں نعمتیں اس کو گوناگوں   پھر نہ جانے کیا ہوا
میوے سے بھر پور تھا   رونقیں تھیں اس پاس   وقت بازی لے گیا
ہمدرد اسکی چھاؤں تھی   رفتہ رفتہ ہوئی گرم جیب تھی   خوشیاں رخصت ہوگئیں
مسافروں کا حبیب تھا   مسرتوں کا دور تھا   آیا وحشتوں کا دور تھا

پھر اک بھول اس سے ہوگئی   پھر کسی کا ساتھ اس کو مل گیا پھر کایا ہی پلٹ گئی
سفر کو وہ نکل پڑا   فردوس بریں تھی ذندگی   بڑھاپے نے سلام کی
تھارا ستے سے بے خبر   نئی اسکی ذات تھی   چاندی بالوں میں آگئی
پر جفا کش اور شکیب تھا   نیا اس کا نام تھا   آیا جدائیوں کا دور تھا

بھولا وہ نادان تھا ۔۔۔۔۔۔ اک روز وہ گاؤں اپنے آ گیا ۔۔۔۔۔۔ زمانہ کروٹ لے گیا
دریا دو تہذیبوں کا ۔۔۔۔۔۔ مہک سوندھی منی کی ۔۔۔۔۔۔ یا خود ہی میں بدل گیا
بہتا درمیان تھا ۔۔۔۔۔۔ پا کر وہ یو کھلا گیا ۔۔۔۔۔۔ میٹھا پانی میرے گاؤں کا
اس کو نہ شعور تھا ۔۔۔۔۔۔ بچپن اپنے گھر کی وہ بھلا گیا ۔۔۔۔۔۔ کھارا کھارا سا ہو گیا

روح کھنڈر بن گئی ۔۔۔۔۔۔ ہائے او میرے لال ۔۔۔۔۔۔ اپنے ہی دیس میں
آنکھ اس کی نم ہوئی ۔۔۔۔۔۔ ماں بولی ماتھا چوم کر ۔۔۔۔۔۔ آبائی گاؤں کھیت میں
کتنا تھی دست تھا ۔۔۔۔۔۔ جوانی کہاں چھوڑ کر ۔۔۔۔۔۔ اپنوں ہی کے درمیان
کچھ نہ اس کے پاس تھا ۔۔۔۔۔۔ میری عمر کو تو آ گیا ۔۔۔۔۔۔ اجنبی کیوں ہو گیا

تنہائیوں کے دشت میں ۔۔۔۔۔۔ اب نہ جانے دوں گی میں ۔۔۔۔۔۔ جانے وہ سوچ میری کدھر گئی
رہتا الگ الگ تھا وہ ۔۔۔۔۔۔ گھر تیرا بساؤں گی ۔۔۔۔۔۔ جو دنیا کو تھی سنوارتی
کوئی نہ اس کا خیر خواہ ۔۔۔۔۔۔ ننھے منے بال تیرے کھلاؤں گی ۔۔۔۔۔۔ اپنی ہی ذات میں
مگر سب کے وہ قریب تھا ۔۔۔۔۔۔ کیوں میری آرزو تو بڑھا گیا ۔۔۔۔۔۔ گم سا میں کیوں ہو گیا

نرالا اس کا خواب تھا ۔۔۔۔۔۔ ماں نے کیا رشتہ اک تلاش تھا ۔۔۔۔۔۔ میں جو آیا لوٹ کے
آغاز جس کا خوشنما ۔۔۔۔۔۔ شادی اس کی ہو گئی ۔۔۔۔۔۔ زمانہ آگے نکل گیا
انجام بیوہ کے نصیب سا ۔۔۔۔۔۔ لڑکی الڑ وہ نادان تھی ۔۔۔۔۔۔ اس آگے پیچھے کے چکر سے
کتنا کڑا ہجر توں کا عذاب تھا ۔۔۔۔۔۔ یہ آدمی تھا چپ چاپ سا ۔۔۔۔۔۔ میں تو ہوں گھبرا گیا

پھر فیصلہ اس نے کیا ۔۔۔۔۔۔ سوچ دونوں کی فرق تھی ۔۔۔۔۔۔ اس آدمی کا نرالا کتنا خواب تھا
وطن کو وہ چل پڑا ۔۔۔۔۔۔ اجنبی اپنے گھر کا ماحول تھا ۔۔۔۔۔۔ آغاز کتنا خوشنما
اپنے ہو نگے منتظر ۔۔۔۔۔۔ خود سے اکثر تھا وہ پوچھتا ۔۔۔۔۔۔ انجام تھا الجھا ہوا
اب آیا اس کو خیال تھا ۔۔۔۔۔۔ محضو یہ کیا ہو گیا ۔۔۔۔۔۔ عمر بھر سہنا ہجر توں کا عذاب تھا

سیماب نیر سید

غزل

اجڑے ہوئے چمن کا باغباں ہونا پڑا

بلبل وصیاد کا رازداں ہونا پڑا

پتوار جن کے ٹوٹے اور طوفان کی نذر ہوئے

ہمیں ان کشتیوں کا بادباں ہونا پڑا

جن کے دم سے رہیں قائم انسانی عظمتیں

ان روایات کا پاسباں ہونا پڑا

غم کی اوڑھے ردا دکھ کی دوپہر میں

گرم ہواؤں کا ساربان ہونا پڑا

دربدر خاک بسر، کو بجو نیّر

بے مہر قافلوں کا نشاں ہونا پڑا

سیاہ نیّر سید

52

عورت

میں جس مٹی سے پہلے بنائی گئی ہوں

بلاآخر اسی میں ملائی گئی ہوں

کبھی جھونپڑی میں کٹی عمر ساری

کبھی تاج محلوں میں دفنائی گئی ہوں

کبھی شہنشاہوں نے زندہ دیوار میں گاڑھا

اور کبھی تخت پر میں بٹھائی گئی ہوں

اور کبھی پتی پر سمنا نبھانے کی خاطر

چتاؤں میں جلائی گئی ہوں

کبھی درد من کے شعروں میں ڈھل کے

غزل ہوں ہوا کے دوش پر سنائی گئی ہوں

اہلِ نظر غور سے تم مجھ کو دیکھو ذرا

اشکوں کی مانند نظر سے گرائی گئی ہوں

میں عورت ہوں اور ہر اک عہد میں نیّر

میں کسی نہ کسی طور ستائی گئی ہوں

سیارہ نیر سید

53

Michael Donalds *aka* Birry

Birry has extensive experience of live performance in a variety of venues. He performs to intimate, small groups and to large audiences, has repeat bookings and gives performances in a wide geographical area as well as on radio.

He has wide experience of working with disadvantaged and disaffected youth, gaining their confidence and trust through the performing arts.

Rage

What burning Rage how bright it glows,
Erupting as a Volcano flows. Engulfing all that stands
before it, consuming life and flora
in an explosion of violence, nature's way to tell its
message.

"Ignore me at your peril for I am Savage"
I respect no borders or classes of mankind,
for my name is "RAGE"
my forms are many, you cannot hide from this
retribution.

I live in men whose souls are angered, for women too,
whose passions are spurned,
in lightning clouds you've seen me strike
as earthquakes hum and tidal waves alike
I am never seen, my presence is every where
my name is
"RAGE"
LOOK OUT "BEWARE"

Oh Emerald Isle

It's my wish to see the people of Ireland live as one
Time to find some love and put down the gun
Stop all this killing, retaliating, Tit for Tat shootings,
I know it's not my business, some of you may say,
but I descend from a race that has suffered too, so I
speak from experience and a history that's true.

Oh Emerald Isle I pray for you and it's my wish to see
you free, much blood has been spilt in your name, do
you think God would ever forgive you if all those souls
were to die in vain ?

Shake off those chains, shackles of ignorance and self
pity, Oh Emerald Isle, your history so entwined with
mine, I find it hard to ignore the parallels that reveal
the time is near for peace to descend upon your
people.

Fear not, Fear Not reach out and shake the hand of
Peace!

**REACH OUT AND SHAKE THE HAND OF
PEACE.**

The Journey

it was hard back then,
but how would I have known
left behind in my hometown
my aunty said I was too young to travel for it was a
distant land a faraway place that they had gone.
I understand now but I didn't then
why did you leave me? I sometimes asked, knowing full
well the time had passed and life was hard back then.

the winters were cold the wind would howl, but you
stayed strong, in the land where you had gone. I know
now how you felt when they said sorry no vacancy.
I imagined you treading in the freezing rain ignoring
the pain chilblain on your feet; fingers numb with cold
for it was hard back then,

raising four children, did you not think about me, was I
not part of the family how could you leave me. I
understand now but I didn't then. I remember the
chimneys' smoke billowing as we came into land,

it was a cold and cloudy September in '66 the ending of
a journey the beginning of a new life in this
land where my parents had gone and yes it was sweet for
the first time my family we all did meet,

all those years of not knowing emotions start
showing, for it was hard back then for all of us, but
how was I to know for my aunty said I was too young to
travel to that distant land a faraway place, they
called England.

**Dedicated to the forgotten children of S.S.Empire
Windrush 1948 and all those left behind in those early
years.**

Sue Brown

One day, in 1994, Sue wrote some notes which someone read and recognised as a poem. She went to a writers workshop and shortly afterwards was invited by Martin Glynn to take part in the Birmingham Readers and Writers Festival – until then she had never seen poetry performed. She has since performed in the UK and Europe alongside Mokape Selassie, Jean 'Binta' Breeze, Kwame Dawes and Linton Kwesi Johnson. Having met a guitarist she started to perform with music. Her poetry is drawn from everyday life and social commentary and is influenced by African history and by her love of jazz and reggae. When her son told his teacher that Mum writes poetry she was invited to share this with the children and has since done workshops in many schools in Birmingham. Her work has been translated into French and is due for publication in France later this year.

One Great Day in Harlem

One great day in Harlem
One jazz moment in time
This powerful imposing picture
Embracing remnants of history makers

Players of instruments assemble
Into an unrehearsed gathering
So conventional yet improvised
To generate a chapter in Harlem

Here featured great revolutionaries
Individuals illustrious jazz artist
In techniques styles and sensitive
An impression to last throughout eternity

The Perils which Love can bring

When tears fall from an ever lasting nightmare
Sorrow is the heart's greatest fear
Love is a gift too often given freely
Without true knowledge of up keep and responsibility

My heart is broken –
Well shattered weak and tender
Not yet fallen into pieces
Which were once held together as new
I'm afraid to even move incase
Another sharp pain erupts my mood so deep and blue
Oh the perils which love can bring

Please call me –
No, not just yet
Instead wait till you hear from me
When time has allowed me
To recover my inner peace
And regain my inner strength
Right now I'm still confused
Quiet sensitive and upset
All my waking moments seems tobe
Caught up in ever lasting distress
Can't eat can't sleep can't concentrate
It's so hard to want to deal with what's left
Wait till I can stand strong in front of you
Without crying sighing making no sense
Perhaps I'll move on and maybe just maybe
Begin to feel good about myself
Oh the perils, the perils which love can bring

Look, now that old scenario taken place
We've allowed love to fall apart

The bowl which held our joyous memories
Has now broken
The bowl of tender loving care
Has been spilled
We broke that which was once whole
Brought about by our actions
Right now I don't know how to cope
Not even how to explain or address the situation
Not only to you – but to myself!

All in One
A poem for Burning Spear

When Burning Spear sings
'Jah is my driver'
Light and energy floods the darkness
The great ancestors
Beat their drums
Guiding the rhythm
In the tune of liberty.

When Burning Spear sings
'People get ready'
In harmony are the
Black Star Liners
Chanting Garvey's philosophy
One Aim One Heart
One Destiny.

When Burning Spear sings
'Do you remember'
Nanny, the queen of the mountains
Sits down upon the rhythm
Kissing her teeth
At all who tried
To conquer in defeat.

When Burning Spear sings
'Ethiopians live it out'
Paul Bogle moves forward
Taking the stand
Emancipation is within
The fittest of the fittest
So sons and daughters live up fully.

When Burning Spear sings
'Afrikan postman'
Word IS Power
Read the telegram
It's time to re-turn
Let us re-member
Do what we can

When Burning Spear sings
'Resting place'
I 'n' I know seh
Door peep can't enter
Know the kingdom's within
Re-focus on the I-Self
Re-connect to the highest frequency.

When Burning Spear sings
'Christopher Columbus'
The whole place lights up
The truth is re-vealed
The air hangs heavy in I-story
So mek de pirates
And buccaneers weep

Respect due
Burning Spear
Knowledge of self
Is to move forward.

Soran M. Hassan

Soran's friendship with poetry began 14 years ago. He knew this would change the direction of his life and he spent his youth this way. In his home country he worked as a journalist and was persecuted for his ideas and his articles. The political/ military parties threatened his life and the possibility of an early death was made known to him. He has been taught by pain and oppression and is still looking for a safe country that will not cast him out. Soran has been seeking asylum in the UK since January 2000.

'A Rosy Dream' (Hilm Wardi) was translated from Arabic by Adil Osman; 'Different Directions', 'Unending' and 'Narrative of a Long Night' were translated from Kurdish in collaboration with Cathy Perry.

Different Directions

I do not understand the mystery
of clouds – like the heart
of an exile poet they are full
of secrets!
Only they know where
they will disgorge – perhaps
they mistrust us
for they do not reveal
their destination.
The high clouds journey;
the water flows below —
they do not grow old
like the fishes in the river,
the river that pours itself out
while the fish forage quietly
in its depths.
Along the banks the green grass
sings of its senescence,
the margin rocks take heed.
Soon the grasses will be dry –
the dust of passing feet
descends upon them
but the river is not muddied nor opaque.

حلم وردي

"أيتها ا"لأنفاس المتقطعة التي التقيتك بلا موعد،
على ضفاف نهر كئيب، عكر،
تجولي في أزقة الجمجمة
حتى يحل موسم الزفاف لمطر الخلود مع براري الوجدان المقشعر الضمآن ..
عندئذ،
لاتلتهمني عقارب الساعة،
ولا أكون فريسة سهلة بين مخالب الزمن،
حيث تنمو في داخلي،
أعشاب جديدة، غير ممنوعة،
فتأكلها حشرات المجاعة،
ومن ثم يطلقن ذاك المارد اللعين، في قوقعة مداركهن..
ليستقر الشر في مقابر العدم!"

66

A Rosy Dream

Oh, the interrupted breathing –
I met you by chance on the banks of a melancholic
and muddy river
I ask you to wander the lanes of the skull
until the arrival of the marriage season
between the rains of immortality and the thirsty
shivering prairies of the psyche.
Henceforth the hands of time shall not devour me –
I shall not be easy prey between the claws of fate
where new grass, unbanned grass will grow inside me.
The locusts will eat that grass,
purge the damned giant from the shells of their intellects
and Evil will settle, forever, into the graves of
nothingness...

ته‌واو نه‌بوون

ده‌رگاکان پێش ئه‌وه‌ی بکرێنه‌وه‌
گوڵاڵه‌کان له‌ پشکووتبوون
جیهانی ئه‌وده‌ی سنووره‌کان
ئامه‌زرۆیی کردنه‌وه‌ی ده‌رگا داخراوه‌کانی
زیاتر کرد
گوڵاڵه‌کان هێشتا به‌ بیداری
په‌بوولانه‌گه‌ شتبوون
له‌ نێوان په‌نجه‌کانی ڕه‌شه‌باوه‌
وه‌کو ماڵئاوایی دایکم له‌ من
هه‌ڵوه‌رین
که‌ سیش دیقه‌تی ساته‌کانی ژاکانی نه‌دان و
بێ ئه‌که‌ نین به‌ گریانی گوڵاڵه‌ گوناهه‌کان
بۆیه‌ به‌ ڕه‌نگی سووره‌وه‌
هه‌موو ساڵێ بۆ چه‌ند ڕۆژێ
خۆیانمان نیشان ئه‌ده‌ن و
تێر به‌ بیداریان گه‌ش نابین ..
ئه‌وان سبیس بوونی گوڵه‌ کانیان دی
له‌ بۆن کردنا
ته‌سلیم بوونی بولبوله‌کانیان دی
له‌ ته‌نه‌زدا
به‌ڵام باخی بوونی ژیزکه‌کان نا ..
ده‌بانه‌ ت‌حه‌ز به‌ بیتی سه‌ر ده‌ره‌ڵنانی ژیزکه‌کان ده‌که‌ین
ساتی مرۆڤ ده‌بینن

68

سەریان دەبەنە وە ناوێ

نهێنی ژێزك و داخرانی دەر گاکان

وەك یەك بوون

دەرگاکان بە کرنە وە یان

قە دەرێك لە گوناهو

موچرکە یەك لە بنی هومێدییان بە خشی

....

گولاڵە کان

لە بەسنە لە کی زستانا

رازەکانی بە هاریان خوێندەوە و.. و

خۆیان بۆ ئارایشت دا

بەلام بە هار وەك وێنە کانی مناڵیم بزر بوو

گولاڵە کایش بە داخراوی مانەوە ..

جوانی یە لكە زێرینە

ئەفسانە یی زەماوەندی

وەرزێكی دەسنە مۆنە کراوی گەیاند

کە هەر بە دوایا رۆشنین و

ئەویش لێمان دوورتر کەوتەوە

69

Unending

Before the opening of the door
the cyclamen are not in bloom.
The world beyond boundaries
increases our desire
to open the door that is closed.
The cyclamen have not met
the butterfly – like the departure
of my Mother with me
they have fallen through the fingers of the wind:
no-one watches their leaving.
The tears of innocent cyclamen are mocked.
Bathed in red they return to us
for a few days each year:
briefly they are in our sight –
we hunger for their return.
They foretell the deaths of other flowers
by their fragrance
foretell the nightingale's surrender
to the cage
but they do not foresee
the defiance of the hedgehog.
If only he would push out his head –
but when he sees us he withdraws again.
The secrecy of the hedgehog is like a closed door.
When the door is opened we share
in the guilt and the shivering of the hopeless.
In the ice of Winter the cyclamen read
the auguries of Spring.
They beautify themselves for it
but the Spring is like

the lost photographs of my childhood
and the cyclamen are unopened still.
In the beauty of the rainbow
lies the fable of freedom's dancing season –
we pursue it
but it eludes us yet.

سەرەبردەی شەوێکی درێژ

شەو داهات
ئەستێرە ئەنیاکان
لە بەرزاییەوە
یاداشتەکان ئەنووسنەوە
ئەستێرەکان
لە بەرزاییەوە
بە بێ دەنگی ئەبریسکێنەوە ....
دار بە رووەقژ بژەکان
رەگە کانیان وشك هەڵات
بۆ رووندکی هەورە دڵڕەقەکان
کە چی هەور هەر داینەکرد
دار بە رووەکان کە بوون بە کێل بۆ ئەو سمۆزانەی
لە شاڵاوی راوچیە درندەکان جێمان
تینووی خوێنی سمۆزە کان نین
دار بە رووەکان لە حەژمە تا
یەك .یەك گریان لە خۆبەردا

ئەستێرەکان بە بێ دەنگی
لە بەرزاییەوە ئەبریسکێنەوە

سمۆزە برسیەکان
لە وێ جێمان

72

هه تا مردن خه ویان به و دیو

ژووره سارده بزگه نه کان و

ده رگا پڕلایه نه کانه وه دی

که روواکیه نه کانی تیا خاموش بوو ...

راوچییه کان لەیانگوت

بۆ سه وزی به مارد

زه ردی هاوین شین دەگێرین

به لام سەوزه کێویه کان خاکی بوون !

شنه با خیانه تی به چناره کان کرد

بووه ره شه با

قاچه کانیانی بریه وه

گه لاکان به نا ئومێدی هه لوه رین و

به نره ختیان له گوت ماڵئاوا.....

ـ چناره کان ـ

نیشتمانی بلَندی

حاجی له قله قه ماندووه کان

منداله کان به هیری

گروگالیان بۆ گولدانه کان کرد

ته مه نیانی تیا روودا بوو

شنه با خیانه تی کرد بووه ره شه با

له گه لْ ئاوینه کانا

گولدانه کانیشی شکان

73

خانە وادەکان

لە بیار تێرامانی مانگدا

گوڵدانە کانیان فرۆشت

کە چی دەسیان هەر نەیگەیشتنێ و

خەویان لێ کەوت

ئەستێرەکان بە بێ دەنگی

لە بەرزاییەوە ئەبریسکێنەوە

لە ژووری سەرجانەکەدا

غەڵبەغەڵبەکە زیادی کرد
لە ژووری بازرگانەکەدا ، غەڵبە غەڵبەکە زیادی کرد ..
چاوی سەمۆرەکان تروسکەی نەما

حاجی لە قڵەقەکان

بە دوای نیشتمانێکی نوێ دا ئەگەڕێن

لێی دەرنەکرێن

هەراو هوریای باڵەخانەکە

جار جارە

گەنجەکە بێدار ئەکاتەوە

کە لە قوڕنەیەکی تەرمیناڵەکەدا

خەوەنووچکەی چاوەڕوانی

ئەیباتەوە

وتیان خۆزیش خیانەتر کرد هەڵنەهات

چاخی شە و کۆتاییی بێنن و

گوڵە بە رێژەکان خەبەر کانەوە ...

74

Narrative of a Long Night

Night is falling
and the single star writing in the heavens
remembers …

> The silence of stars
> shining from the heavens

The oak tree's hair is unkempt,
its roots parched
by stony-hearted clouds
whose teardrops never fall.
The oaks are become
monuments for the squirrels
who ran before the hunter's cries –
the trees do not thirst
for squirrels' blood.
In their passion the oaks
have burnt themselves,
one by one.

> The stars silently from the
> heavens shining

Hungry squirrels are left there
until they die, dreaming
of what lies outside
the cold and putrid room,
iron-doored, lights extinguished.
The hunters say:
We bring comfort in the green of spring
and the yellow of summer,
but the wild squirrels are grey.

The breeze deceives the cypress
while the wind cuts off its leg
and leaves fall, hopeless,
without farewell to the tree –
that high roost of a tired stork.

Children crawl
towards the vase
where their age was grown
but the breeze deceived and was the wind
and the vase, like the mirror, is cracked.

Families
considering the moon
sell the flower vase
but their hands cannot reach the moon
and they have been dreaming.

>Stars silently from
>the heavens shining

In the jail
the noise increases …
in the trading room
the noise increases …
but the light in the squirrel's eye is gone
and the stork seeks a new country
where no-one will cast him out.

In the corner of the terminal,
drifting in the sleep of waiting,
the babble of the building
disturbs this young man's thoughts
saying:

The sun has deceived you –
it will not rise again
until this century of night is ended
and the sunflowers may raise their heads once more.

Alline Yap-Morris

'Miss Kitty' is a Jamaican-born mother of six who came to England to join her mother in 1961 when she was only eighteen. Being of mixed heritage she is appreciative of the problems some of the children in GB have to face.

Her poetic inspiration comes through the media, the mind's eye or through the influence of friends or loved ones. The diversity of themes are from the impact of events in her life. This creativity is not limited to poetry as she also writes short 'skits', some in Jamaican dialect or 'Patois'. Her greatest aspiration is to have some of her work acknowledged worldwide. Despite shunning publicity she would someday like to read her pieces with the same amount of conviction with which she writes.

She is fearful that our children are gradually losing their true identity and are missing out on the sweetness of life in the West Indies as handed down by our forefathers and mothers who gave us an identity second to none. By capturing these stories we can use the written word to hand our tradition down, a legacy to our children ... who are strangers in a strange land.

Strangers in a strange land
(But look pon we now)

Windrush in the Fifties
Slowed down by the Sixties
Good improvement, but not enough
Integration and all that stuff.

We came with great expectation
But it took complete renovation
To the way 'they' perceived us,
Just wanted to be accepted without fuss,
Away from the Teddy Boys with toilet chains and flick
knives.
Now we can charm them with musical vibes.

Cool Runnings showed what we are made of
An football made the Reggae Boyz show their stuff
"Come on Youthman, yuh born fe win
Killing and cruelty to yuh brethren is a sin
Not because yuh deh ah Englan
Yuh can still prove dat yuh come from
A proud and strong nation!"

The Phoenix

Like a phoenix rising up from the ashes
To the top of a hill in Mandeville
A heavenly retreat that has now become my home
I am at last at peace, I am calm, serene.
From my home near reaching clouds
I stand secure as far as eye can see
There's God's beauty all around me.
Nature works in perfect harmony
Chorus of crickets, toads and grasshoppers
Summon the rainfall to provide lush green fauna.

I wake up in the stillness of the day or night
To the sounds of blue tits, yellow birds and woodpeckers
Look across the windswept trees
To witness butterflies as they tickle and tantalise the
leaves.
There is beauty all around me: my heart is full of pride
See the lilies and the daffodils standing majestically
Over the roses and Joseph's coat of many colours.
In this my heavenly retreat, there's no time to put up feet
For when the pottering's done I sit back with a bottle of
rum
And calmly think of those I've left behind on England's
glorious shore
Midst all that snow and ice and as I sip once more
The pleasure's mine I'm sure when I say "Ah, that's
nice!"

Feel the Sun

Understand our culture, understand our ways.
To scores of would-be followers it's just a craze
Feelings so innate, feelings come from within the soul
The winds that blow round the island shore,
Whistle through the trees forming, nourishing every part
of you
Making you whole
Oh, Jamaica, my island home.
Look around, breathe the air, 'Feel The Sun'.

You have to admit, Jamaicans are pioneers, worldwide
Commanding nuff, nuff respect
In achievements great and small.
You name it Jamaicans have tried them all.

Island in the sun
I crave the beauty of your sun blessed shores
Where the seas caress your silver sands
And lovers serenade in moonlight bliss
And cherish each long and tender kiss.

Ghost Town to Newtown

How many ghost towns must there be
Recognise the poverty
Questions going round in mind
How many more will one find
Streets that once felt the footsteps of happy shoppers
Anxious to come again to buy their tempting wares.
Rundown, derelict shops that brimmed with profits from
the past.
Investments they once thought would last.

Take me through those streets once more
To Jamaica's Old Kingston town
To recall the joy once felt at Christmas time,
Gently mingle with the crowd: feel excitement surging
round.
Each stall was full, so full of tempting toys for happy
girls and boys
A tug on Mother's skirt, glee in eye as each gift she
bought
Was added to the already bulging bags.
Listen to the shouts of vendors bartering wares
'Star light amusing light. Get yuh star lite amusing lite!'

Stalls that stretched from North to South Parade
Right past Coke Memorial to Ward Theatre at North
Parade
Where Maggie and Putus once played
Past the Sally Army Church down Orange Street
To the bottom of West Parade, where taxis, buses wait.
All de hustle and bustle was just great, great, great!
Meck me teck yuh back a lickle more
To the tramcar widout no door
An Johncoonu used to frighten lickle pickeney.
Jumping , prancing all around, shh – don't meck no
sound!

Remember Maddah Lundey, Mah Mud, Sea Cow an Bun
Down Cross Road?

Put fun 'n' joke aside
Take Jamaicans from far and wide
Each and every one of us have yearnings
To go back to dem yard fe rest dem bones.
But are faced with dangers that are painful to see
With loyalties at heart they have had to depart
Being turned off crime and avoidable poverty from the
start.
These questions arise in each bleeding heart
What can we as natives do to elevate the poor and
deflated ones
Who have given up on themselves and us.
Permiate the minds of leaders of our State
Let them realise that for us to return is gain.
Make it safe for tourists, preserve the trade
To keep them coming – our livelihood will then saved!

Ras Joseph

Joseph started writing at the age of seven and was encouraged by his Church young peoples group. He is now a social worker and also plays with the band 'Ujima', an Ashanti word meaning 'collective works and responsibilities'. He is influenced by the writings of prophets and seers and by the passion in the ancient writings of his Rastafarian faith. In his own writing Joseph uses his experiences of life as part of a sub-culture and as part of a multicultural society. He believes that the Black Nation doesn't really have a voice but that it needs to get on with other people and nations. No-one likes criticism but Joseph believes it is his duty to tell the truth, whether people like what they hear or not, and to try and make the world a better place – somewhere his dreams can become reality.

Forgiveness

We have to prepare ourselves to forgive – it will be our
future passage
Through difficult times ahead
By means of self discipline our children must be lead and
taught
That God will take vengeance over injustice Himself
We have to prepare ourselves to forgive so that we can be
forgiven
And be there for our children and teach them the passage
to True Life that is hidden
We have to prepare ourselves to forgive when the war is
ended – so in
Peacetime it should be a privilege – the Human Race we
are defending –
Shoulder to shoulder, side by side, even when it becomes
a rough ride.
We have to prepare ourselves to forgive, a lot of our
children are becoming fugitives
It's their blood that is in the streets –
To forgive, humble pie we must eat, it could be your
child next week.
We have to prepare ourselves to forgive it will be our
future passage
Through difficult times ahead.

Seal and Sign

Seal and sign, seal and sign,
Seal and sign, seal and sign,
Sealed by the Father, seal and sign,
Sealed by the Son, seal and sign,
Sealed by the Holy Spirit, seal and sign,
Seal and sign, seal and sign,
Sealed with Love, seal and sign,
Sealed with Peace, seal and sign,
Sealed with Joy, seal and sign,
Seal and sign, seal and sign.

It's a Crime

Darkness fills the sky
That's the time, it seems, crimes multiply
Hopeless people, never considered to give love a try
They look on as crimes multiply.
Skin colour – everyone is so righteous about their culture
And forgetting to love each other.
Crime multiplies.
Children don't want to go to school
So they end up being fools
That's the time crime multiplies
Fathers leave their homes,
Women and children are left alone
Moving from hostel to residential homes
That's the time, it seems, crimes multiply.
Mothers working hard to give their children a start –
That's the time it seems crimes multiply.
Sons and daughters that feel their Mothers' hurt
That's the time it seems crimes multiply.
The moon and stars bear witness
They see the crime multiply.

The Warning

The Warning has ended
And the time has come
When Babylon will have to run
Right here inna England
I will not write a single word
Unless I have a reason
So search not for any sweet words
Of love and beauty.

The Warning has ended
Our families have already been offended
Young ones are born recruited
Ready to live or die
The Warning has ended
And the Laws of Moses have been implemented.
No more Warning
It's eye for eye and teet for teet
You are now confronted
By youths in the streets
All because you refused to hear
The Warning has ended.

What Then?

This ain't got nothing to do with Black and White
This has something to do with Wrong and Right
The books of history should serve as a beacon of light
To magnify the Truths and Rights.

This ain't got nothing to do with Black and White
This has something to do with Wrong and Right
We are all a product of Time
The True Earth Race is
Not really hard to find
There is only one rainbow in the sky with so many
colours combined
This is the voice of conscience telling you to teach your
children to be kind

This ain't got nothing to do with Black and White
This has something to do with Wrong and Right

Kalpana Ganguly

Kalpana was born in Kenya, brought up in Uganda and after residing in various parts of the world has finally settled in England. In East Africa she was a teacher. At present, apart from being a full time civil servant, she is involved in a variety of voluntary work. Kalpana was an amateur actor in Uganda and Kenya. Among her literary pursuits love for poetry reigns supreme. She is a member of The Cannon Poets and started the women-only group 'Combination' who meet once a month at her residence.

Help/Debt?

You hypocritical Hounds
Your hypocrisy knows no bounds
Promising disarmament
Knowing weapons will find their way
Encouraging corrupt regimes
Turning a blind eye
To starvation and repatriation
Your convenient ignorance
Your hypocrisy turned to apathy
Big Brother, O Big Brother
Promising elimination of poverty
Promising prosperity
Helping-LENDING to little nations
Nothing for them has ever got easier
To them, only resort left is crime and corruption
Allow in this jungle of civilisation
Some honesty
Let us drop hypocrisy
Show them our magnanimity
Eradicate greed
Let's just keep need
Let the millennium see us as one family
Eating from one big pot
Let the year 2000
Be free of World Debt.

Indian Widow

I will wrap my chastity in a white sari
Sister, do not preach to me hypocrisy
Fragrance of his love
Keeps me chaste
I will wear green and red
And all the bridal colour
Sister, let me shout out loud
I am his eternal bride
I will not be disabled
With your out-dated tradition
With my red bridal gown
I will keep trespassers at bay
I will not sit with my eyes downcast
I will keep my wits about
Colour white alone will not keep me chaste
Bridal colours are my protection
They will keep away temptation
Let me breathe a new tradition
Let this widow adorn
Herself with bridal gown
Let her love keep her chaste.

Softly awakens my heart

Love whispers in the silence of the night
Love rustles in the golden leaves of autumn
Love glistens in the dew-drops
Love murmurs in the streams and brooks
Love sings in the robin's song
Love's lyrics are in the dawn and dusk
Love beams through moonlit-sky
Love glides in the rustling wind
Music of nature transports
me to gone by days
with the promise of Love's awakening.

Home is ...

East or West they say
'Home is best'.
When I went to Rome
it brought memories home
of yester years.
Standing in St Peter's Square:

I saw the grandeur
as splendid as that of the
Golden Temple of Amritsar

Breathtaking beauty
of Niagara Falls
in the incomparable
Victoria Falls
yet there can be
no comparison –
each awe inspiring vision
gives equal pleasure

The splendour of the Taj Mahal
and glory of St Paul's Cathedral
giving equal pride to architecture.
In majestic Himalayas I see
the captivating beauty of Kilimanjaro –
seeing Ben Nevis gives
me the same thrill.

Foetus killing in India,
abandoning babies in
'Living Graves' in China,
are but the *ugly faces* of motherhood
same in India as in China.

Pure and holy are the waters of Avon
same as Ganges and Yamuna –

Why the boundaries
then of yours and mine?
when I am gone
rest me on the banks of Avon
for Home is where
the heart is.

Martin Underwood

Born in the south of England he has lived in Birmingham longer than anywhere else. He is a graduate of the Open University. He has written poetry for many years and is a member of The Cannon Poets.

'Beginning Again' was a runner-up in the 2000 Houseman Society competition.

Beginning again

Some homecoming –
We knew the way, of course,
Though it was painful.
In the fields, the cattle
Were not where we left them
And the barns were burnt.
We found a few chickens
Wandering in the woods
Who came hurrying to our call-
But the cat did not.

The roof is intact, for the moment.
But half the windows are gone.
A written guarantee of safety
Is no guarantee of life.
We have new neighbours now.

I don't want to remain.
But we must, we must.
In the emptied living room
The boards are stained and black.
We don't know what happened
But nothing will shift it.
After dark fear creeps from the woods.
It seeps through the broken glass
And under the blankets.

And something heavy down the well
Is blocking the bucket's drop.

Feeding the pigeons – Soho Road

They know the time of day,
Begin to hang about in groups,
Nod to each other, but keep a sideways watch –
And at her appearance sweep down
From the sooty rooftops all around –
A plethora of wings all at once apparent,
Steel grey, cloud grey, pearl grey,
All with the sheen of new annealed metal
Flapping down to populate the grass at her feet.

Her brown hands broadcast crusts and scraps.
She stands unmindful of passers-by,
The noise of the crowded road.
Absorbed in the manoeuverings about her sandalled feet,
The hurried marching to and fro,
Their sleek necks opalescent in the brief sun.
She knows the stranger and the regular
The bully, and the ones who need some calculated luck
To feed at all.

For a brief time this site –
Cleared and abandoned, tussocked with weeds,
Two concrete benches, broken, graffiti'd
Rubbish blowing and drifted –
Blossoms as she stands apart from the world
Like the saint, ministering to the attentive birds,
Creating each day a new and oblivious stillness
Beside the noisy thoroughfare.
Recalling each day her native home
And there the glittering pigeons
-The souls of the newly-dead –
Rising and wheeling into the over-arching blue
Above the sacred river at Benares.

Iron Man
(New Street Birmingham)

Slammed me shut in iron
Thrust me seven leagues deep.
I fought back to light
But gravity caught me by the heels.
So I lean at an angle to this world
In the last frustrated effort to get out.
One day my bands will rust away.

I stand till then listing –
A mute intruder darkening the thoroughfare
Enduring the mouthings of little people:
"What is it?" "I don't like it."
"What's it meant to be?" "How should I know?"

I am not 'meant' to be:-
I AM.
Gagged with steel I bear
The seasons and all weathers -
The pigeons I cannot brush from my head,
The dogs that halt by me,
The demeanings of unthinking people.
A writhing mind silenced,
Absorbing all into a hopeless body.

When the last bond breaks
I shall astonish you all.
I shall tramp to the end of the street
Leaving my footprints in the paving stones.

Is that what you are afraid of?

Kampta Karran

Kampta is from Guyana. He is currently a lecturer in Community, Play and Youthwork and is programme leader of the Race and Ethnic Studies Programme at the University of Birmingham, Westhill Campus.

Advice

Maa … a wha dey in me plate?

Nothing Balgobin

Na cry maa you sacrifice full me belly
But you tears a mek me tusty like Kali
Fu de blood a deese de-maans
Who a gee a bee deese lay-ba pains
A bee gat fu stap dis SHIT na maa?

Empty plate or full grave
One way or de otha
'Memba wha Krishna bin tell Arjuna
Do wah you gat fu do bay taa

Wuk Man

Wuk man wuk
E wuk e wuk
Til e han an e foot bruk
Wuk man wuk
E wuk e wuk
Til e cork duck

Wuk man wait
E wait e wait
Cussing e poe fate
Wuk man wait
E wait e wait
Till e life dis-inte-grate

Wuk man dic-tay-ta
Dic-tay-ta wuk man
In con-fron-tation
Wuk man an moe wuk man
You fu-cha day in you han
Memba good life na go come
Till dic-tay-ta-ship gane

Stap wuk an plan wuk man
Stap wuk and plan
You gat fu free up dis lan

Fite Man

Vasu dewa kut am ba kam
Wuk man pickney get dam vex
Otha people a inherit dem parents sweat
Dis a hut dem bad bad bad
Dem throw back an punda and dem get mad
Vasu dewa kut am ba kam

How lang wuk man gat fu mine
De ole higue pickney of pantomine
Wuk man wuk dem wuk an dem plan
Wuk man pickney tun fite man
Wid cut-lass shap-een all two side
Dem sid down a dem doe mouth
To guard dem pride
Vasu dewa kut am ba kam

Fite man vision plain as day
Unity and justice de only way
Arjuna, Joshua and Jihad
Fire pan Ba-be-lan
Bun dem Gad
Vasu dewa kut am ba kam

Wuk man pickney in de street
Solida buss dem head an bruk dem feet
Wid two argans gane dem na give up
Liberation lies in dem arm an dem gut
Vasu dewa kut am ba kam

Wuk man pickney gut in arm
Olc haigue scream in great alarm
Bitta bullet scramble knat
Ole higue dead crass fite man lap
Vasu dewa kut am ba kam

Story Time

Daddy, daddy tell me wan story. De sheep are tired and
the goat dem angry. Abee down pan abee luck.
Nineteen-wa-you-call-am is like wan lang hungry
Christmas. Dat man wid de mike say is de dawn of a
new day but fu who get wuk yet receive no pay is moe
like a comedy of error dan de birth of a new era.

Pickney, me talk in me mind, you na know wa you ask
you fadda to do. Sooner or later day bound to be trouble
in de pen. Sheep an goat na know how nor when. Lion
an tiger waiting just outside. De moment de war break
dem go capture de prize. Mutiny an bounty go hand in
hand specially when de booty rich an princely grand.

Daddy, daddy tell me bout Cinderella or Tota Mina.
Frighten me wid Freddie or mek me cry wid Dosti. Betta
still read me a poem wid a happy ending. Tick-an-na-ro-
ga is way too sad. De Stuart and de Cameron, two
murdering clans, killing fu nothing … deer's e-nuff fu
all. Peter Grimes will neva do. Captain Cruel step
children crew, died, homi-cide-nied, a psycopathic brew.

De story dat is coming is too morbid, too clear, is too
apocalyptic fu you innocent ear. As such it is me duty, I
must admit, to suffa it to silence, a secret's secret. Na
pressure me love to unravel dis mystery. Your innocence
is precious. Madonna's penalty.

Probably pa-paa, in de line of poetry, King John an de
Abbot of Canter-bury a go suit de mood: a whimsical
king, a happy, helpless priest an a humble shepherd.
Dish out some story an feed it to me. Dis silence you
living is very unhealthy. If not fu you self den do it fu
you dul-arie. Wid no money, no nice close, me cyan go
pan de road; dem children a muck me an turn up dem

104

nose. Come na pita-ji, save us both, tek out de small book and unburden dis load.

Ah wa wrang wid dis chile, me soliloquize. Me karma deh pan trial, me grah to neutralize. Me story hard. Ah guava season in all abee nay-bah yard. Cow a butt, bruck-up han an foot. Belly tink troat gane abraad. Some dead. Some gane mad. Natty dread tun ball head. Justice an tyranny ah court mattie company. Like pan abee alone dis rain a fall. Ow Bhagwan. Help wan, help all.

Story time daad. No TV: no Young an Ress-less. No radio: no Girl fram Susanburgh. Abee cyan afford modernization. Leh abee retreat to de oral tradition. Muj-hay ake ka-ha-nee baap. Muj-hay ake ka-ha-nee.

A-write, a-write, me heart release. No God. Pain an pieces. Know God. Perpetual peace. I done me fite. Me na fit fu wan na-da strike. Me eye too weak, me foot na move, me mouth na speak, me hand cyan hole, you ole man even loose he gut control. Still wan wan ditty cause am dam. Cack-a-roached conscience masquerades man.

Jal

Wuk man tek wan day aff
Time he an Ganga Ma have wan lil gaff
Watch a blue sky an a smiling sun
Breeze or no breeze
Ancestral journey na no fun
Koka dam tree dem prapa green
Gangees ... Demerara
Blood an waa taa ... Ganga Maa taa
Tek aff he doo tee
Lie naked pan de mud
Jal say jee wan: touch of Gad

Griot is Writers Without Borders' second book. We are planning further publications, performances and workshops.

We are very interested to hear from writers who would like to be involved, particularly if you have come to the UK as a refugee or asylum seeker and/ or want to get to know writers from other cultures.

Cathy Perry,
22, Margaret Grove, Harborne, Birmingham B17 9JH

May 2001